W9-BVL-950

THE
PRIMARY SOURCE LIBRARY
OF
FAMOUS ARTISTS ™

PABLO PICASSO

Catherine Nichols

The Rosen Publishing Group's
PowerKids Press ™
PRIMARY SOURCE

New York

For Pablo, pug of my heart

Published in 2006 by The Rosen Publishing Group, Inc.
29 East 21st Street, New York, NY 10010

First Edition

Editor: Kathy Kuhtz Campbell
Book Design: Emily Muschinske
Photo Researcher: Sherri Liberman

Photo Credits: Cover (left) © Geoffrey Clements/Corbis, (right) © Hulton-Deutsch Collection/Corbis; title page, p. 5 © Réunion des Musées Nationaux/Art Resource, NY; p. 4 © Erich Lessing/Art Resource, NY; pp. 6 (left), 10 (right), 23 ON-LINE PICASSO PROJECT (Dr. Enrique Mallen, Director)/© Estate of Pablo Picasso/Artists Rights Society (ARS), New York; p. 6 (top right) © Giraudon/Bridgeman Art Library, (bottom right) © Artists Rights Society (ARS), New York/Art Resource, NY; p. 8 (left) Index/Bridgeman Art Library, (right) © Artists Rights Society (ARS), New York/Giraudon/Art Resource, NY; p. 10 (left) Index/Bridgeman Art Library; p. 12 (left) National Gallery, London, UK/Bridgeman Art Library, (right) © Artists Rights Society (ARS), New York /Réunion des Musées Nationaux/Art Resource, NY; p. 14 Pushkin Museum, Moscow, Russia/Bridgeman Art Library; p. 16 © ARS, NY/Digital Image © The Museum of Modern Art/Licensed by SCALA/Art Resource, NY; p. 17 © Giraudon/Bridgeman Art Library; p. 18 (left) Kunstsammlung Nordrhein-Westfalen, Dusseldorf/Giraudon/Bridgeman Art Library, (right) © Fitzwilliam Museum, University of Cambridge/Bridgeman Art Library; p. 20 (top) © Private Collection/Archives Charmet/Bridgeman Art Library, (bottom) © Réunion des Musées Nationaux/Art Resource, NY; p. 22 Lauros/Giraudon/Bridgeman Art Library; p. 24 (top and bottom) © Archivo Iconografico, S.A./Corbis; p. 26 (top) Private Collection/Bridgeman Art Library, (bottom) © Hulton Archive/Getty Images; p. 28 (top) © Réunion des Musées Nationaux/Art Resource, NY, (bottom) Private Collection/Roger-Viollet/Bridgeman Art Library.

Library of Congress Cataloging-in-Publication Data

Nichols, Catherine.
Pablo Picasso / Catherine Nichols.
    p. cm. — (The primary source library of famous artists)
Summary: Discusses the life and work of innovative artist Pablo Picasso.
Includes bibliographical references and index.
ISBN 1-4042-2764-4 (Library Binding)
1. Picasso, Pablo, 1881–1973—Juvenile literature. 2. Artists—France—Biography—Juvenile literature. [1. Picasso, Pablo, 1881–1973. 2. Artists.] I. Title. II. Series.
N6853.P5 N53 2005
709'.2—dc22

2003019934

Manufactured in the United States of America

Contents

1 The Great Experimenter   5

2 An Artist from the Start   7

3 Going Forward   9

4 A Visit to Paris   11

5 Blue Paintings   13

6 Pink Paintings   15

7 *Les Demoiselles d'Avignon*   17

8 Painting with Shapes   19

9 Sad Times   21

10 A World of Dreams   23

11 *Guernica*   25

12 Working Through the War   27

13 Working Up to the End   29

Timeline   30

Glossary   31

Index   32

Primary Sources   32

Web Sites   32

Pablo Picasso made this self-portrait, or painting of himself, in the spring of 1907. At that time he was studying African sculptures and creating a new art style called Cubism.

The Great Experimenter

Many people consider Pablo Picasso the most important artist of the twentieth century. In the early 1900s, most artists painted objects as they really looked. The more real the subjects in their paintings looked, the better. Since his boyhood in Spain, Picasso could skillfully paint objects as they actually looked. By the time he was in his twenties, however, he was experimenting with different art **styles**. He

This 1907 photo shows Picasso in Paris, France.

decided to present the subjects of his paintings in a new way. He wanted to show the subject from several different angles at once. Because the image in the painting looked as if it was broken into little cubes, the style became known as **Cubism**.

Picasso experimented with different art styles all his life. He had made many paintings, **sculptures**, drawings, **etchings**, and pottery by the time of his death at age 91.

Top: *In 1896, Picasso painted this picture of his mother, María Picasso López.*

Bottom: *He painted this picture of his father, José Ruiz Blasco, in 1896.*

Above: *Pablo Ruiz y Picasso painted this picture when he was about eight years old. It shows a horseman at a bullfight.*

An Artist from the Start

Pablo Ruiz y Picasso was born on October 25, 1881, in Málaga, in southern Spain. His father was José Ruiz Blasco and his mother was María Picasso López. Pablo showed his talent as an artist at a very young age. His first word was *lapiz*, which is Spanish for "pencil." By age four, he was making careful drawings of the world around him. Later, Picasso claimed that he "never did any childish drawings." It probably helped that his father was an art teacher.

When Pablo was 10 his father moved the family, which now included Pablo's two sisters, Conchita and Lola, to La Coruña, Spain. Pablo's father took a job teaching art in a school in this port city. In 1892, Pablo enrolled at the school where his father taught. In his art classes Pablo did better than the other students and received excellent grades on his final tests.

Above: Fifteen-year-old Picasso painted this picture, titled Self-Portrait, in 1896. In 1972, his friend Manuel Pallarès, who had known him in Barcelona, said that when Picasso was young he seemed and acted much older than his age.

Picasso painted First Communion in 1896. As models for this work he used his sister Lola, his father, and, as an altar boy, a family friend. The picture shows the Roman Catholic religious service honoring the Last Supper of Jesus and his followers.

Going Forward

In 1895, Picasso's sister Conchita died of an illness. The family was feeling very sad. Soon after, Picasso's father applied for a job at a school in Barcelona. Picasso attended Barcelona's School of Fine Arts. To take the more advanced classes, Picasso had to pass tests in drawing. These tests usually took one month to complete, but Picasso did them in one day. He was accepted as a student in the advanced classes. Picasso's painting *First Communion*, which he made in 1896 to honor his sister Lola's First Communion, was shown at an art **exhibition** in Barcelona. His painting *Science and Charity* won an award in 1897 in a national exhibition in Madrid.

When he was 16, Picasso took a trip into the village of Horta de Ebro with his friend Manuel Pallarès. They stayed in the village for eight months. Picasso had never lived in the country before. They also camped in the mountains nearby, sleeping under the stars. Picasso learned about farming from the people of the village.

4GATS

MENESTRA

Left: *In Barcelona Picasso met a group of artists at a café named Els Quatre Gats, or the Four Cats. Picasso tried to make a living by creating posters and menus, such as the one shown here from 1899.*

Right: *Around 1900, Picasso painted this portrait of his best friend, Carles Casagemas, who was a writer and a painter.*

After he met Fernande Olivier in 1904, Picasso started to paint in pink colors. The pink colors he used were warmer than the blues that he had used earlier. Picasso painted The Family of Saltimbanques in 1905. Saltimbanques are traveling jugglers and other circus performers.

A Visit to Paris

Picasso entered Madrid's Royal Academy of San Fernando in 1897. Although the school was respected, Picasso found it too **traditional**. He did not want to copy paintings done by famous artists of the past. He wanted to create his own art. Picasso left school and rented an apartment in Barcelona with his best friend Carles Casagemas. The young men were very poor.

When he was almost 19, Picasso visited Paris, France, with Casagemas. At that time, Paris was an important center for artists. Picasso visited galleries, which are rooms that show works of art, and museums. Museums are places where a collection of art or historical items are safely kept for people to see and study. Picasso saw the paintings of the **Impressionists**, such as Claude Monet.

Picasso liked Paris but decided to return to Spain. Back in Madrid, he received news that his friend Casagemas had died. The style of Picasso's paintings changed because he was upset about his friend's death.

Above: *In 1904, Picasso lived in a poor neighborhood in a part of Paris called Montmartre. This 1904 photo shows him at the Place de Ravignan in his neighborhood.*

Left: *He painted* Child with a Dove *in 1901. This picture shows the sad and tender feelings Picasso experienced after the death of Casagemas.*

Blue Paintings

Between 1901 and 1904, Picasso moved between Barcelona and Paris. He went to Paris twice, in May 1901 and in October 1902. Both times he lived in **poverty**. He rented cheap, poorly heated apartments. All the while Picasso continued to paint. What made his work unusual during this time was that he painted using only shades of blue. The color blue gave his paintings a gloomy look. So did his subject matter. At this time, Picasso painted people who looked unhappy or troubled, such as *The Old Guitarist*. Many art critics, the people who write their opinions about art, and **art dealers** did not like these paintings. They wanted him to go back to painting as he had before. Picasso, however, knew he could not paint what other people wanted. He had to stay true to himself.

Art Smarts

Near the end of 1901, when Picasso returned to Barcelona, he began his so-called Blue Period paintings. Not only did the color of his works change during this time, but also he started to sign his paintings "Picasso" instead of "P. Ruiz Picasso." One of the first blue paintings he made was titled *Child with a Dove*.

Pink Paintings

Picasso returned briefly to Barcelona and painted many paintings in a short time. By 1904, he was back in Paris. He rented a room in which he could work, called a studio. His studio was in a building that people called the *Bateau Lavoir*, or Floating Laundry. It was known as the Floating Laundry because it looked like the boats where laundrywomen washed clothes. Picasso joined a group of artists and writers who also rented rooms there.

One summer day in 1904, Picasso met Fernande Olivier, who was to become his first great love. Suddenly the world seemed sunnier to him. Almost immediately after meeting her, the colors that Picasso used in his paintings changed. He used more pink than blue in his work. "Pink" is the word *rose* in French, so many people call this time Picasso's Rose Period. Between 1904 and 1906, he created many paintings in shades of pink. His subjects changed, too. He now painted people who performed in the circus.

Les Demoiselles d'Avignon

This is a wood-and-horn mask from Africa.

Picasso's pink paintings began to sell for more and more money. Critics and art dealers liked his cheerful works better than his sad blue paintings. Picasso, never satisfied with one way of painting, continued to experiment. In 1907, he was hard at work on a painting that was very different from other paintings. *Les Demoiselles d'Avignon* (*The Girls of Avignon*) did not . follow the rules of **perspective**. He broke down the images of five women into shapes that curved inward or outward. He knew his painting would shock the art world, so he did not try to sell it. Instead he showed the painting to friends. They did not like it. One friend even said the painting was "the work of a madman." Today most people believe that this painting helped change the history of modern art.

Today Picasso's Les Demoiselles d'Avignon *is considered to be one of the most important paintings in modern art. When he painted it in 1907, he did not follow the usual ideas of beauty and balance in painting. The women's heads look like African masks. The bodies have shapes that look similar to broken glass.*

Left: *This painting done by Picasso in 1909–10 is titled Head of a Woman. It may be showing Fernande Olivier. Picasso shows the figure broken up into different shapes with angles.*

Right: *Picasso painted* Portrait of Fernande Olivier *in 1909. Between the spring and fall of 1909, he painted more than 60 pictures of Olivier. In Cubism, he used geometric shapes to show empty and filled space in pictures.*

Painting with Shapes

In 1907, Picasso met Georges Braque, a French artist. Both men were interested in painting a subject from more than one angle in the same picture. They tried breaking up images into **geometric** shapes. The two men became friends and decided to work together. Critic Louis Vauxcelles saw Braque's work in 1908 and described it by using the word "cubist." Soon the art style that Braque and Picasso started became known as Cubism.

Art Smarts

Picasso and Braque were the first modern artists to use the art form of collage. The word comes from the French word *coller*, which means "to glue." To make a collage, an artist pastes objects onto paper or canvas. *Still Life with Chair Caning* is an early collage by Picasso.

By 1911, Picasso and Fernande Olivier were no longer together. That year Picasso met Eva Gouel Humbert, who became his girlfriend. He began adding nicknames for Humbert into paintings. By 1912, he was adding more than words. He glued other items, such as cuttings from newspapers, string, labels, sand, and nails, to his work.

Above: *This is a color print of the stage curtain that Picasso created for Parade. He made the curtain and print around 1917.*

Right: *Picasso wrote this letter to his friend André Salmon, who wrote poems, on May 6, 1915. Picasso always wanted peace. He stayed in Paris and painted during most of World War I.*

Sad Times

World War I broke out in Europe in 1914. Great Britain, France, the United States, and their friends, who were on one side, fought Germany, Austria-Hungary, and their friends, who were on the other side. Picasso saw many of his fellow artists, such as Braque, join the fighting. Picasso chose not to fight, staying in Paris for most of the war. At this time, Eva Humbert became sick. Doctors discovered that she had tuberculosis, an illness that affects the lungs. In 1915, Humbert died.

Picasso did not produce as much art as usual because he was so sad. Then, around 1916, he met Jean Cocteau, a French poet and playwright. A playwright is a person who writes stories that are acted onstage. Cocteau talked Picasso into creating the scenery, or painted settings, and costumes for *Parade*. *Parade* was a **ballet** about a circus sideshow. The ballet was presented in Paris in May 1917. People who saw it did not like it. The ballet was too modern and shocked them.

Picasso created The Three Musicians *in 1921. He included some Cubist features, such as geometric patterns and collagelike cutouts. His playful treatment of the subject suggests an early interest in the world of dreams.*

A World of Dreams

While working on the ballet *Parade*, Picasso met Olga Kokhlova, a dancer in the ballet. Picasso fell in love with her. They married in July 1918, four months before World War I ended. Their son, Paulo, was born in 1921. Picasso was happy with his new life as a husband and a father. The Picassos moved into a large apartment in a nice part of Paris.

Ballerina Olga Kokhlova met Picasso while dancing in Parade.

In the early 1920s, Picasso became interested in a movement called **Surrealism**. The writers and artists in this movement were interested in the world of dreams. Picasso used some of their ideas about dreams in his 1921 *The Three Musicians* and his 1925 *Studio with Plaster Cast*.

Picasso and Olga were no longer happy together. They separated in 1935. He and his new girlfriend, Marie-Thérèse Walter, had a daughter, Maya, later that year. He lived with his new family for about one year.

Above: Guernica *shows the suffering of those who were harmed in 1937 in the town of Guernica in northern Spain. Picasso made the painting in shades of black, white, and gray, which are the colors of newsprint. He wanted the painting to look like a newspaper report on the horrors of war.*

Right: *Picasso made this drawing as a study of a face for* Guernica. *When people saw the final painting, they praised it, although many were troubled by the scary images.*

Guernica

In 1936, Picasso's homeland, Spain, was fighting a civil war. A civil war is a war between two sides in the same country. A general in the Spanish army, Francisco Franco, led a fight against Spain's **Republican** government. Germany helped General Franco. On April 26, 1937, German airplanes attacked the Spanish town of Guernica. Many people lost their lives in the attack. The killings angered people around the world, including Picasso. The Republicans asked him to create a painting about the attack for the Spanish display at the world's fair in Paris. Picasso worked on the painting from May 1 to June 4, 1937. He made many drawings before he began to paint. Picasso made paper cutouts of his drawings and moved them around the **canvas** to find the best composition. This means that he had to arrange the painting's elements, such as colors, lines, and shapes, to make a balanced whole. When he found a composition that satisfied him, he began to paint *Guernica*.

Above: *In July 1940, German troops marched down a Paris avenue called the Champs-Élysées after taking over the city.*

Right: *During World War II and after, Picasso worked on sculptures and pottery such as the plate with a man's face shown here. He continued to make paintings, drawings, and prints.*

Working Through the War

World War II began in 1939. This war was fought by the United States, Great Britain, France, and Russia against Germany, Japan, and Italy until 1945. In 1940, Germans marched into France and soon had taken over Paris. For most of the war, Picasso remained in Paris. For many people he came to stand for freedom. It was hard to work during the war. Buying art supplies was hard, because few could be found. Picasso's studio was often cold, because of coal shortages. Still, he continued to paint, even when a bullet came through his window and just missed wounding him.

During this time Picasso created sculptures with objects he had in his studio. Once he used a bicycle seat and handlebars to make a bull's head. Later he had *Head of a Bull* **cast** in metal.

Art Smarts

Picasso worked in many art forms besides sculpting and painting. While living in the south of France, he produced many fine pieces of ceramics, a type of pottery. He also created etchings and lithographs. These are prints made from wood, stone, metal, or glass plates that have images cut into them.

Above: This photo shows Picasso in the Madoura pottery workshop in Vallauris, France, in 1952. From 1947 to 1971, the owners of this workshop let him make ceramics there whenever he wanted.

Right: Picasso is shown here in the 1950s in his studio in Vallauris. He made this giant ceramic pitcher.

Working Up to the End

Picasso met artist Françoise Gilot in 1943. They fell in love. In 1948, they moved to Vallauris in the south of France. The couple had two children together, Claude in 1947 and Paloma in 1949. Gilot and Picasso's time together was not happy. In 1953, when Picasso was 71, Gilot and the children left him. Picasso was upset to lose his family. However, the following year, he met Jacqueline Roque in a pottery gallery. After his first wife, Olga, died in 1961, Picasso married Roque.

Picasso continued to work, often painting late into the night and rising early the next morning to return to work. On April 8, 1973, at age 91, Pablo Picasso died. He left behind more than 1,800 paintings, 1,200 sculptures, 2,800 pieces of ceramics, 18,000 prints, and many drawings. Most people believe he was the greatest artist of the twentieth century.

Timeline

1881	Pablo Ruiz y Picasso is born in Málaga, Spain, on October 25.
1895	He enrolls in the School of Fine Arts in Barcelona.
1900	Picasso visits Paris, France.
1901	He begins his Blue Period, creating sad paintings in blue colors.
1904	Picasso moves into the Floating Laundry. He meets Fernande Olivier.
1904–06	Picasso enters his Rose Period, painting pictures using shades of rose, or pink.
1907	He paints *Les Demoiselles d'Avignon.*
1908	Picasso begins the Cubism movement with Georges Braque.
1911	Picasso meets Eva Gouel Humbert.
1915	Eva Gouel Humbert dies from tuberculosis.
1917	Picasso creates a set and costumes for *Parade.* He meets Olga Kokhlova.
1918	He marries Kokhlova.
1921	The Picassos' son, Paulo, is born.
1935	Picasso and Olga separate. Picasso and Marie-Thérèse Walter's daughter, Maya, is born.
1937	He paints *Guernica.*
1947	Picasso and Françoise Gilot's son, Claude, is born.
1948	Picasso moves to the south of France.
1949	His daughter Paloma is born.
1961	He marries Jacqueline Roque.
1973	Pablo Picasso dies in Mougins, France, on April 8.

Glossary

art dealers (ART DEE-lurz) People who buy and sell pieces of art.

ballet (BA-lay) A kind of dance that uses music and stage sets to tell a story.

canvas (KAN-ves) A cloth surface that is used for a painting.

cast (KAST) To shape something by putting soft metal into a mold.

Cubism (KYOO-bih-zim) An artistic style that tries to make familiar objects look strange by showing several different sides at once.

etchings (ECH-ingz) Pictures of prints made from plates that have images cut into them.

exhibition (ek-sih-BIH-shun) A public show of works of art.

geometric (jee-uh-MEH-trik) Having to do with straight lines, circles, and other simple shapes.

Impressionists (im-PREH-shuh-nists) Artists who follow Impressionism, a style of painting started in France in the 1860s. These artists tried to paint their subjects showing the effects of sunlight on things at different times of the day and in different seasons.

perspective (per-SPEK-tiv) In a work of art, the way objects are shown in relation to each other. Distant objects are made smaller than nearer ones.

poverty (PAH-ver-tee) Being poor.

Republican (rih-PUH-blih-ken) Having to do with a party that believes government power should rest with people elected by citizens.

sculptures (SKULP-cherz) Figures that are made by cutting stone or wood, or are formed by modeling clay or casting in metal.

styles (STYLZ) The certain manners or methods in which works of art are painted or made.

Surrealism (suh-REE-uh-lih-zem) A movement in art and literature based on fantasy. The artists and writers of this movement used their dreams and imagination to create works of art.

traditional (truh-DIH-shuh-nul) Usual; done in a way that has been passed down over time.

Index

A
art dealers, 13, 17

B
Bateau Lavoir, 15
Blasco, José Ruiz (father), 7
Braque, Georges, 19, 21

C
Casagemas, Carles, 11
ceramics, 29
Cocteau, Jean, 21
critics, 13, 17
Cubism, 5, 19

D
drawing(s), 5

E
etching(s), 5

F
First Communion, 9
Franco, Francisco, 25

G
Gilot, Françoise, 29
Guernica, 25

H
Head of a Bull, 27
Humbert, Eva Gouel, 19, 21

I
Impressionists, 11

K
Kokhlova, Olga, 23, 29

L
Les Demoiselles d'Avignon, 17
López, María Picasso, 7

O
Old Guitarist, The, 13
Olivier, Fernande, 15, 19

P
Pallarés, Manuel, 9
Parade, 21, 23
Paris, France, 11, 13, 23, 27

R
Roque, Jacqueline, 29
Rose Period, 15
Royal Academy of San Fernando, 11

S
School of Fine Arts, 9
Science and Charity, 9
Studio with Plaster Cast, 23
Surrealism, 23

V
Vallauris, France, 29
Vauxcelles, Louis, 19

W
Walter, Marie-Thérèse, 23
World War I, 21
World War II, 27

Primary Sources

Cover. Left. Detail of Pablo Picasso's *Girl Before a Mirror*, which he painted in 1932. The woman in the painting is Marie-Thérèse Walter, one of Picasso's girlfriends. Museum of Modern Art, New York. **Right.** Portrait of Picasso, photographed in September 1955. **Page 4.** *Self-portrait*, painted by Picasso in spring 1907. National Gallery, Prague, Czech Republic. **Page 5.** Photo of Picasso, taken in his studio at Bateau Lavoir, Paris, around 1907. Musée Picasso, Paris, France. **Page 6. Left.** *Le Picador*, painted by young Picasso in 1889–1890, in Málaga, Spain. A picador is the horseman in a bullfight who wounds a bull's neck so that the bull will tend to keep its head low for the rest of the bullfight. **Top.** *María Picasso López, The Artist's Mother*, drawn by Picasso with pastels on paper in 1896. Museo Picasso, Barcelona, Spain. **Bottom.** *Portrait of the Artist's Father, Don José Ruiz Blasco*, made in 1896. Museo Picasso, Barcelona. **Page 10. Left.** Menu from Els Quatre Gats, which Picasso created for the café Els Quatre Gats two years after it opened in Barcelona. It is believed to be the first work for which Picasso was paid. **Right.** *Portrait of Carles Casagemas*, oil on canvas, painted by Picasso in 1899–1900. Museo Picasso, Barcelona. **Page 12. Left.** *Child with a Dove*, painted by Picasso in 1901, is believed to be one of the artist's first Blue Period paintings. National Gallery, London, England. **Right.** Photo of Pablo Picasso at Montmartre, place de Ravignan, Paris, around 1904. Picasso is seen here in the neighborhood of the Bateau Lavoir studio. **Page 14.** *The Family of Saltimbanques* was painted in 1905 when Picasso focused his work on circus performers. It is believed that his inspiration for the theme came from the performances of the Cirque Médrano, a circus that played in Montmartre, Paris. **Page 16.** *Les Demoiselles d'Avignon*, which Picasso painted in 1907, was considered to be a turning point in his work. In size the canvas is 8 feet (2.4 m) by 7 ½ feet (2.3 m) and shows Picasso's interest in African art. Many art historians believe this painting changed the direction of modern art. Museum of Modern Art, New York. **Page 20. Top.** "Theater Curtain for *Parade*," ca. 1917. Color lithograph. **Bottom.** Picasso's letter to André Salmon, a friend, May 6, 1915. **Page 24.** Picasso's *Guernica*, a painting more than 11 feet (3.3 m) high and 25 feet (8 m) wide, was exhibited inside the entrance to the Spanish Pavilion at the 1937 World's Fair in Paris.

Web Sites

Due to the changing nature of Internet links, PowerKids Press has developed an online list of Web sites related to the subject of this book. This site is updated regularly. Please use this link to access the list: www.powerkidslinks.com/psla/picasso/